Looking at Light

Catherine Stephens

PICTURE CREDITS
Cover (front), Jimmy Chin/National Geographic Image Collection; 1, 12, 18 (bottom left), 25 (top right), 30 (bottom left), 35 (top), Photodisc Green/Getty Images; 2-3, Tony Craddock/Photo Researchers, Inc.; 4 (top left), 8, 25 (top left), 28 (left; monitor), Royalty-Free/Corbis; 4-5 (top right), George D. Lepp/Photo Researchers, Inc.; 4-5 (bottom), 31 (middle left), Ron Watts/Corbis; 6-7, Taxi/Getty Images; 9, 34 (second from top), Joel Sartore/National Geographic Image Collection; 13, 25 (bottom left), 30 (bottom right), 35 (second from top), SIU/Visuals Unlimited; 15, 19 (top), Stone/Getty Images; 16-17, Keith Kent/Photo Researchers, Inc.; 19 (bottom), Gordon Garradd/Photo Researchers, Inc.; 20-21, 23, 31 (top right), 35 (bottom), Norbert Rosing/National Geographic Image Collection; 22, 34 (top), Joel W. Rogers/Corbis; 26 (top), Ted Horowitz/Corbis; 26 (bottom), 31 (middle right), Royalty-Free/Comstock Images; 27, Doug Martin/Photo Researchers, Inc.; 28 (monitor inset), Martyn F. Chillmaid/Photo Researchers, Inc.; 28 (monitor inset detail), Alan Towse, Ecoscene/Corbis; 29, Reuters/Corbis; 30 (top left), Tom & Dee Ann McCarthy/Corbis; 30 (top right), O'Brien Productions/Corbis; 32, TEK Image/Photo Researchers, Inc.

Produced through the worldwide resources of the National Geographic Society, John M. Fahey, Jr., President and Chief Executive Officer; Gilbert M. Grosvenor, Chairman of the Board; Nina D. Hoffman, Executive Vice President and President, Books and Education Publishing Group.

PREPARED BY NATIONAL GEOGRAPHIC SCHOOL PUBLISHING
Ericka Markman, Senior Vice President and President, Children's Books and Education Publishing Group; Steve Mico, Senior Vice President, Editorial Director, Publisher; Francis Downey, Executive Editor; Richard Easby, Editorial Manager; Bea Jackson, Director of Layout and Design; Jim Hiscott, Design Manager; Cynthia Olson, Art Director; Margaret Sidlosky, Illustrations Director; Matt Wascavage, Manager of Publishing Services; Sean Philpotts, Jane Ponton, Production Managers; Ted Tucker, Production Specialist.

MANUFACTURING AND QUALITY CONTROL
Christopher A. Liedel, Chief Financial Officer; Phillip L. Schlosser, Director; Clifton M. Brown III, Manager

CONSULTANT AND REVIEWER
Jordan D. Marché II, Ph.D., University of Wisconsin–Madison

BOOK DEVELOPMENT
Amy Sarver

BOOK DESIGN/PHOTO RESEARCH
3R1 Group, Inc.

◀ The sun is the source of daylight.

Contents

Published by the National Geographic Society
1145 17th Street N.W.
Washington, D.C. 20036-4688

ISBN: 0-7922-5438-4

2010   2009   2008
      4 5 6 7 8 9 10 11 12 13 14 15

Printed in Canada.

Light Make

▼ A lamp lets the girl work at night.

▼ Sunlight lets plants grow.

Light is an amazing part of our world. Without it, you would not be able to see. Light lets you work at night. Light allows plants to grow. Light brightens everything in your world.

Look at the pictures.
- What light do you see in each picture?
- How is light important in each picture?

▼ **Light brightens the city.**

Big Idea
Light travels from different sources and is made of colors.

Set Purpose
Learn what light is and why objects are colorful.

Questions You Will Explore

What makes light?

How does light travel?

What Is Light?

Take a look around you. What do you see? You probably see people and objects. You see different shapes and colors. What lets you see so many things? Light!

Light comes into your eyes and allows you to see. Light is important. Yet you probably never think about it. Well, that is about to change.

In this book, you will learn what light is. You will find out where light comes from. You will also discover that light is made of colors.

◀ Lights brighten a city at night.

▲ **Light from the sun allows plants to grow.**

Light From the Sun

Light comes from different sources. Most light comes from the sun. The sun is far away. But it is powerful.

Without the sun, plants would not grow. Without plants, there would be no food. The sun's light and heat warm Earth. People could not live on Earth without light and heat from the sun.

▲ **Electricity powers lights in the city.**

Light at Night

What happens at night when there is no sunlight? People have found ways to make light. Long ago, people used fire for light at night. People lit candles and lanterns to light their homes. Later, people discovered how to use **electricity**. Electricity is a form of energy that people use for power. Today, electricity powers lights. Electric lights brighten homes, streets, and cities.

···

electricity – a form of energy that people use for power

9

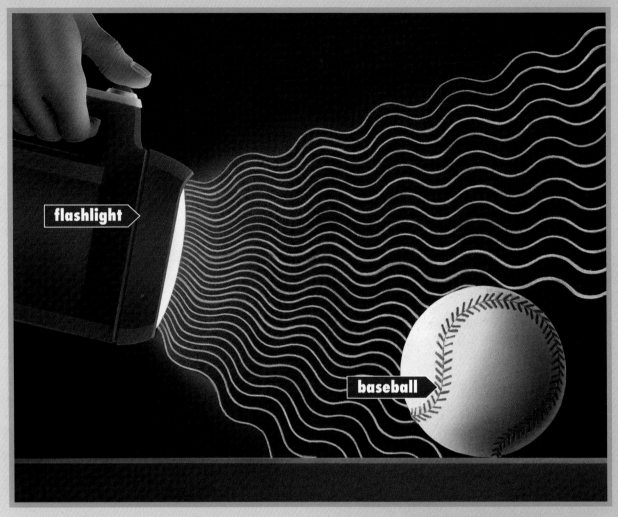

▲ **Light waves travel out from the flashlight.**

Light Travels in Waves

Light is always on the move. Light travels out from its source. Light moves in waves. We cannot see the waves. But they are all around us.

Look at the picture. It shows waves of light. These waves travel out from the flashlight. The lightbulb in the flashlight is the source of light.

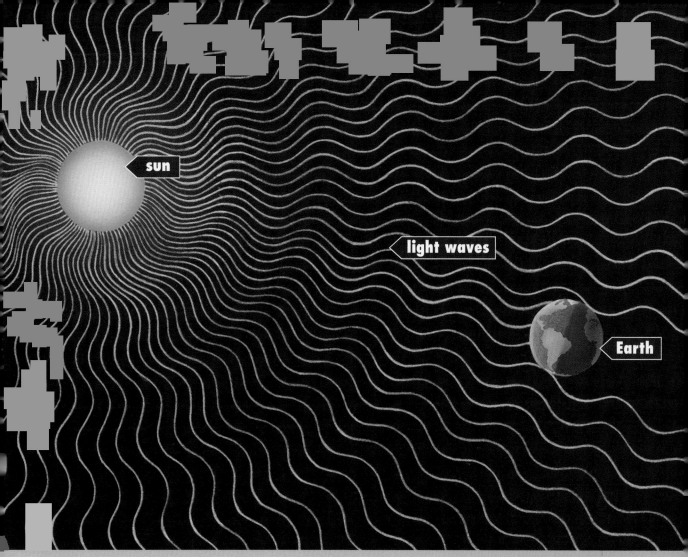

▲ Light waves take eight minutes to travel from the sun to Earth.

The Speed of Light

Light moves very quickly. It is the fastest thing in the universe. Light waves travel through space at 300,000 kilometers (186,000 miles) per second. Yet it still takes time for light to travel. Light from the sun takes about eight minutes to reach Earth. That is because the sun is very far away from Earth.

▲ A mirror reflects light from its surface.

Light Bounces

What happens when light waves hit an object? Some light is absorbed, or taken in, by the object. Other light bounces off the object. This process is called **reflection.**

Reflection allows you to see things. First, light bounces off an object. The light then enters your eye. This reflected light allows you to see the object.

....
reflection – the change in direction of light waves when they bounce off an object

◀ **Light waves bend and change direction as they enter and leave the water. That is why the pencil appears broken.**

Light Bends

Light waves pass through some things. They can move through water and glass. As light waves move from one material into another, they bend and change direction. This is called **refraction.**

Light waves travel at different speeds through different materials. For example, light waves move faster through air than through water. So when light waves enter water, they slow down. This makes them bend and change direction.

....
refraction – the bending of light waves as they pass through different materials

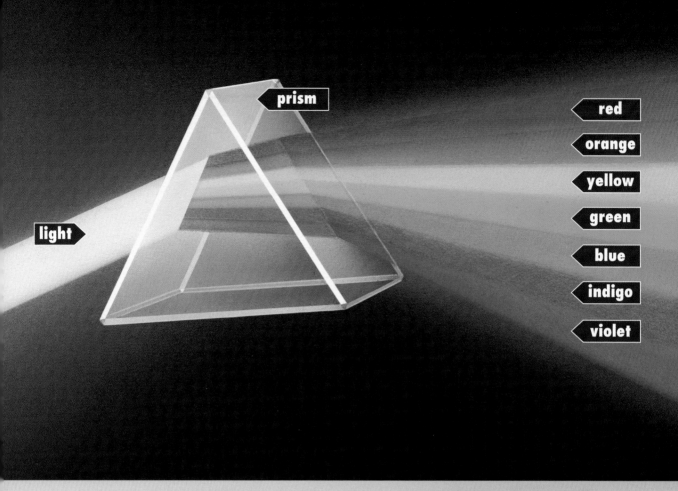

prism

light

red
orange
yellow
green
blue
indigo
violet

▲ A prism spreads out light into its colors.

A Rainbow of Colors

Light waves act in amazing ways. But that is not all that is interesting about light. Light is made of colors.

Scientist Isaac Newton showed that light is made of different colors. He passed a beam of sunlight through a piece of glass called a **prism**. The prism spread out the light into a band of colors. The colors were red, orange, yellow, green, blue, indigo, and violet—the colors of a rainbow.

··

prism – a piece of glass that spreads light into its colors

green light

red light

▲ Grass looks green because green light waves bounce off grass. The ball looks red because red light waves bounce off the ball.

Why Do We See Colors?

The colors in the world around you come from light. Look at the picture. Why does the ball look red? The ball absorbs all the colors in light except red. Only red light waves bounce off the ball and back to your eyes. So the ball looks red. The grass looks green because the grass absorbs all the colors in light except green. Only green light waves bounce off the grass and back to your eyes. All the colors you see are caused by the bouncing of light waves.

Stop and Think!

Why do objects look colorful?

Recap
Explain how light makes
objects look colorful.

Set Purpose
Learn how light makes
colors in the sky.

Colo

ors in the Sky

Think about painting a picture of the sky. What colors would you use? Maybe you would paint a blue sky. Or maybe you would paint the reds and yellows of sunset. Sometimes the sky dazzles us with a colorful light show. Why is the sky so colorful?

Why Is the Sky Blue?

It is a sunny day. The sky looks blue. Why? Light waves from the sun hit air **particles** in the sky. This makes the light waves **scatter,** or spread out. The colors of light scatter in different ways. Blue light scatters more easily than other colors when it hits air particles. So your eye sees more blue light. That is why the sky looks blue.

particle – a very small object

scatter – to spread out

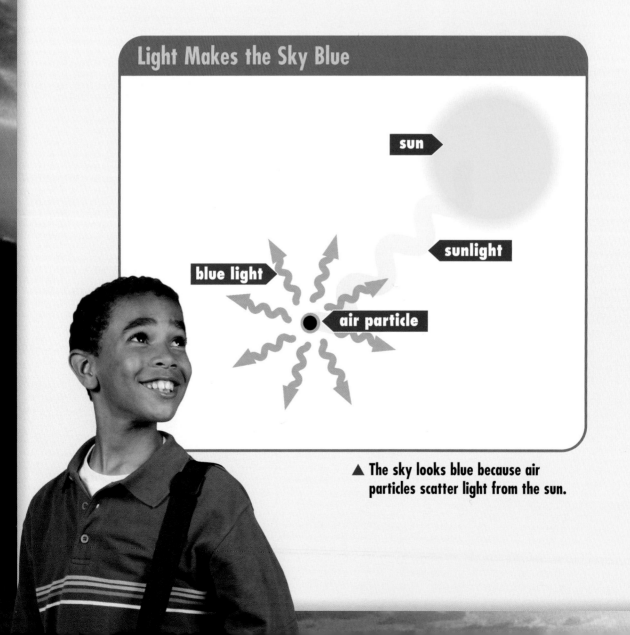

Light Makes the Sky Blue

sun

sunlight

blue light

air particle

▲ The sky looks blue because air particles scatter light from the sun.

Blue Sky, Red Sky

At sunset, sunlight moves differently through the air. The light waves hit air particles at a different angle. The blue light waves bounce upwards off of the air particles. But now you see the red light waves that are not scattered. This makes the sky look red.

▲ **The sky looks blue during the day.**

▲ **The sky looks red at sunset.**

Rainbows

A rainbow can fill the sky with colors. A rainbow happens when there is rain and sunshine. Sunlight shines upon the raindrops. A raindrop acts like a prism. Sunlight enters each drop. Then the light is spread into colors. The colors bounce off the back of each drop. Then they travel to your eyes. This makes a band of color called a rainbow.

▼ **When light enters a raindrop, the light spreads out into a rainbow of colors.**

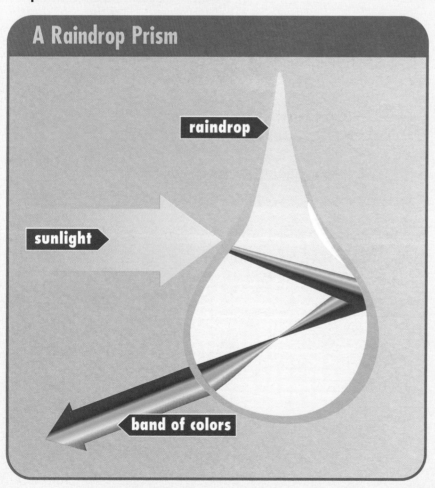

A Raindrop Prism

raindrop

sunlight

band of colors

The End of a Rainbow?

Rainbows often look like a colorful curve in the sky. The colors seem to start and end near the land. Yet rainbows do not have a beginning near land. They are really parts of circles. You do not see the whole circle. That is because the land gets in the way of the rainbow.

▼ **A rainbow is part of a circle.**

Colors in Clouds

Have you ever seen colors in a cloud? Some clouds are made of tiny water drops that are all the same size. These drops can bend light waves. Each color of light bends differently around the drops. This can show you the colors of a rainbow.

▼ Sunlight bends around the water drops in this cloud. This makes the cloud look very colorful.

Sundogs

When it is cold, clouds are made of ice **crystals.** These crystals can refract light waves. Sometimes sunlight passes through the ice crystals and bends in two directions. This makes two colorful spots of light appear near the sun. These spots of light are called **sundogs.**

....

crystal – a natural material having flat sides and fixed angles

sundog – a spot of light that appears in the sky when light bends through ice crystals

Stop and Think!

What causes colors in the sky?

▼ Sundogs are two bright spots of light that appear near the sun.

sundog

sundog

Recap
Explain how a rainbow forms.

Set Purpose
Read these articles to learn more about light.

Looking at Light

You see the world because of light. Light is a form of energy. Light travels in waves.

Here are some ideas you learned about light.

- Light comes from the sun and other sources.
- Light reflects when it bounces off an object.
- Light refracts when it moves from one material to another.
- Light is made of colors.

Check What You Have Learned

What does each photo show about light?

▲ The sun is a source of light.

▲ Light reflects off the mirror.

▲ Light refracts when it moves from air into water or glass.

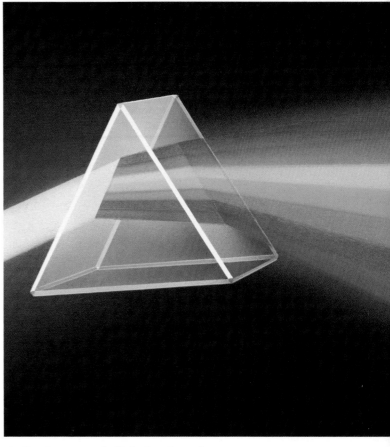

▲ A prism spreads light into its colors.

What Are Shadows?

A shadow is an area where light is blocked. Shadows form when light bumps into an object and cannot pass through it. For example, light cannot pass through an animal's body. So its body makes a shadow.

You can make shadows. Shine a flashlight on a wall. Block the light with your hands. When you move your hands, you change the shape of the shadows.

▲ The lizard's body makes a shadow.

▲ These dog shapes are shadows made by two hands.

Seeing the Big Picture

Look at the worm under the magnifying glass. It looks larger than its actual size. That is because a magnifying glass has a piece of curved glass called a lens. When light waves pass through a lens, they bend. This makes the object under the magnifying glass look larger than it really is.

▼ The magnifying glass bends light. It makes the worm look bigger than it really is.

computer screen

▲ Tiny dots of light make up the pictures on computer and TV screens.

TVs and Computers

Televisions and computers use light to make pictures on their screens. The pictures look solid. But they are really made of tiny dots of light. Each dot can appear in many different colors on the screen.

Televisions and computers display rows of colorful dots. The dots are very tiny and close together. The dots can change very quickly. So your eyes see these dots as moving pictures.

Solar Cars

A solar car uses light to move. It has solar cells that change light into electricity. When light strikes a solar cell, special materials in the cell absorb some of the light. These materials change light into electricity. The electricity powers the car.

▼ **Solar-powered race cars**

solar cells

29

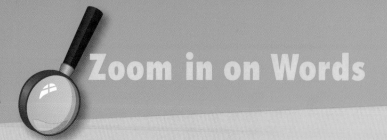
Many kinds of words are used in this book. Here you will learn about verbs. You will also learn about nouns.

Verbs

Verbs are words that show action. Find the verbs below. Then use each verb in your own sentence.

The balls **scatter** when they are hit.

The students **look** through the bus window.

Light **bounces** off the mirror.

Light **bends** as it moves from the air into the water.

Nouns

Nouns are words that name people, places, or things. Find the nouns below. Then use each noun in your own sentence.

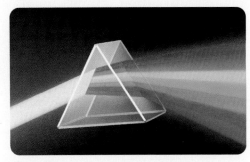

A **prism** spreads sunlight into bands of colors.

A **rainbow** curves across the sky.

You can see the **reflection** of the city lights in the water.

A **shadow** forms when light is blocked.

Light travels in **waves.**

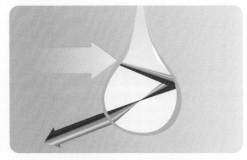

A **raindrop** can bend light.

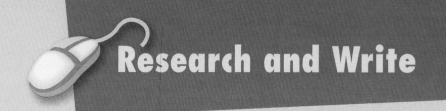

Research and Write

Write About Light

Research how light refracts as it moves from one material to another. Then write a paragraph telling what you learned.

Research

Fill a large glass bowl with water. Tape a piece of dark construction paper over the end of the flashlight. Make a small hole near the center of the paper.

Test and Take Notes

Make the room dark. Shine the light from the flashlight into the water. Look at the way the light bends. Draw a picture of what you see.

Write

Write a paragraph that describes what you saw. Explain why the light moved the way it did. Share your paragraph and drawing with other people in your class.

Read and Compare

Read More About Light

Find and read other books about light. As you read, think about these questions.

- What is light?
- How does light move?
- How do scientists learn more about light?

Books to Read

▲ Read about the energy of light and sound.

▲ Read about different forms of energy at work in our world.

▲ Read about how people use electricity for light and power.

Glossary

crystal (page 23)

A natural material having flat sides and fixed angles

Ice crystals form clouds.

electricity (page 9)

A form of energy that people use for power

People use electricity for lights in the city.

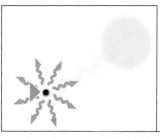

particle (page 18)

A very small object

Light hits air particles in the sky.

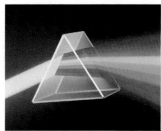

prism (page 14)

A piece of glass that spreads light into its colors

The prism bends light and shows colors.

KEY CONCEPT

KEY CONCEPT

reflection (page 12)
The change in direction of light waves when they bounce off an object
The mirror shows the reflection of the girl.

refraction (page 13)
The bending of light waves as they pass through different materials
Refraction of light causes the pencil to appear broken.

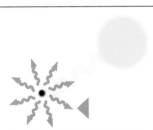

scatter (page 18)
To spread out
Light scatters when it hits air particles.

sundog (page 23)
A spot of light that appears in the sky when light bends through ice crystals
A sundog appears in the sky on each side of the sun.

Index